The Rugs

By RL Lane

The Rugs…

They lie…there

They see…it all

They collect…the dust

They cushion…the fall

They cover…the floor

They hide…it all

Sweep it under the rug!

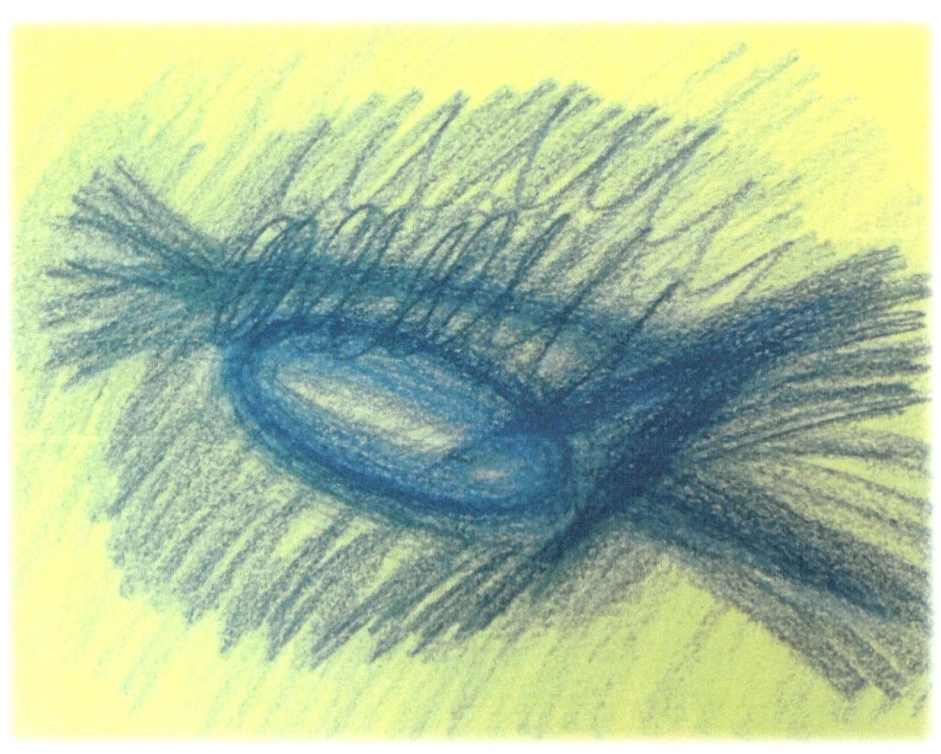

"Not sure what these rugs mean", she texted back…

It was the third one…

The first one was a red oriental rug. I couldn't see anything else.
I just knew that someone loved that red oriental rug…

Then the second appeared. A solid dark burgundy one. There
was a pattern with big teardrops that formed the shapes of flowers. I
told her maybe someone was sad…

They held the burgundy rug like it was standing up, so I could see it. Then this last one. It was brown with a pattern of creams or whites. I could see an old chair in the room to my left. It had light colored wooden arms and a cushioned seat. I think there was a lamp next to it. I knew a woman used to sit in that chair…

They were all area rugs. I thought a lot about them and then it finally connected…

Those rugs do get walked all over a lot…

Only one rug stood up. There were three of them, but yet only one stood up…

Whether you believe in my rug messages or not, it is true. The statistic is probably even accurate. One in every three of us will let the others walk all over us. Oh no. It is the other way. Only one in every three of us will stand up for ourselves…

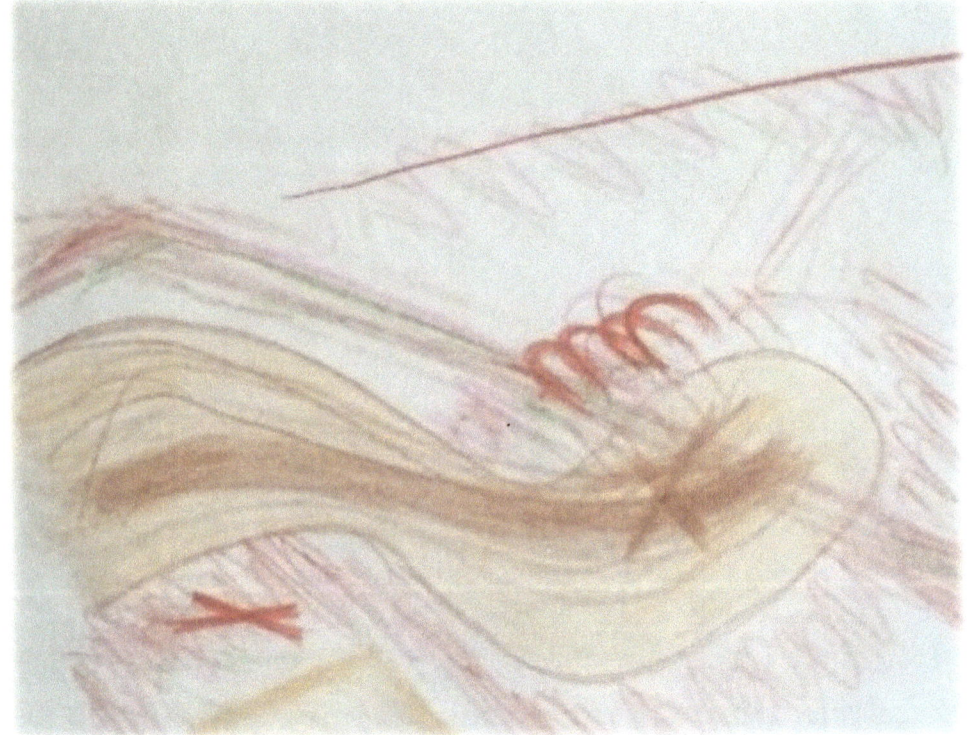

The ones standing up are the ones who have to help the others…

No one should be left on the floor…

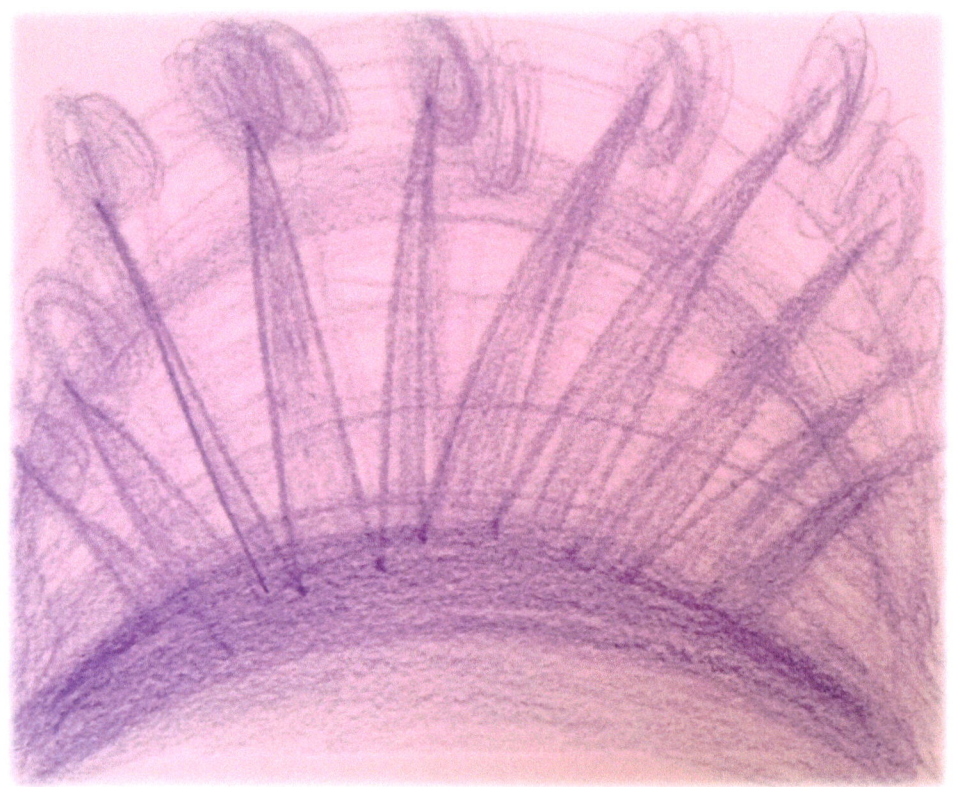

I was thinking about the rooms he had shown me recently. One was a kitchen, with an old white sink across the room. It had two deep basins…

The other was just a room he had stayed in at the end of his life. Tony the typesetter. Why did he send me the sink? Are both he and his…my Mom trying to remind me to be clean? I doubt it…

The water runs out of the sink…

Think think

About the sink

Why the sink?

Why not a cupboard or refrigerator?

What am I missing?

It must be important…

A sink is used to wash food or dishes

A sink used to be for getting drinking water…

We mostly drink bottled or delivered spring water now

The tap is no longer good enough for us…

Oh. The tap…

The beer on tap and whatever else those bars serve

Oh. The tap dancing…

Click click shuffle shuffle see how fast you can make a beat with your feet

Oh. The tap music…

The song at the end.

I do not know if Tony the typesetter got to hear Taps as they lowered his body to the ground and his angel wings appeared…

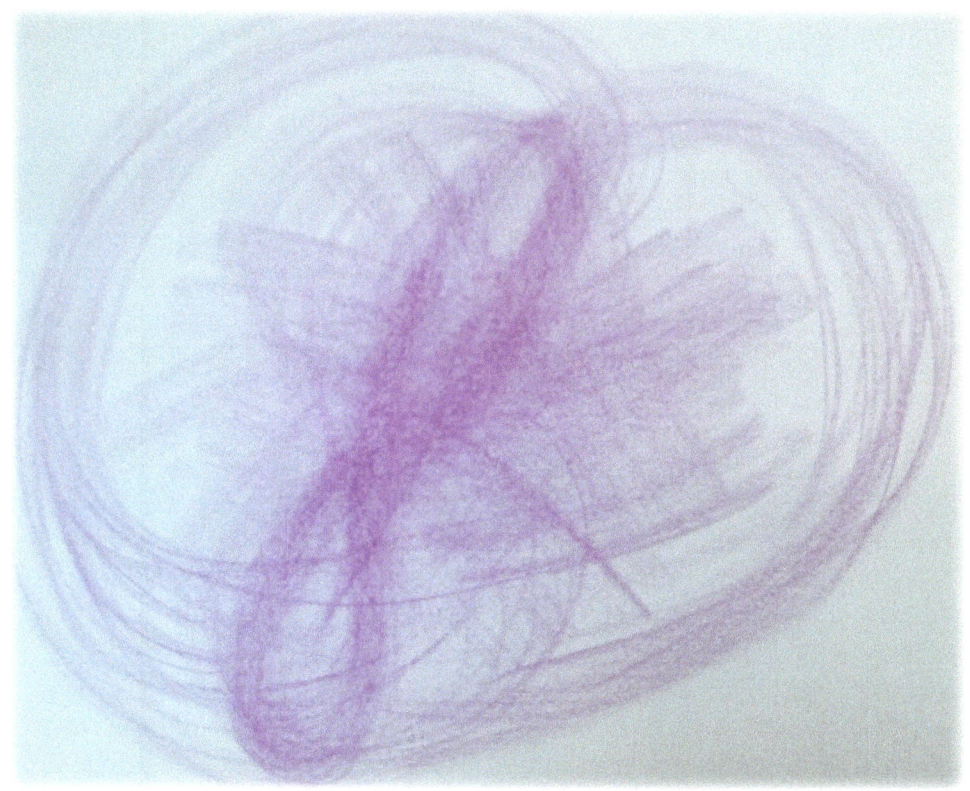

"You cannot change what you have done," they said.

That was the message to "No Lines to Erase". I had used its document to write this one and this was on the page right after writing about Taps. I left it hear...here because I thought it was appropriate and a good message to hear again...

I know that sink means something. I had recently drawn the time capsule sinking but I don't think that is the message of this book…

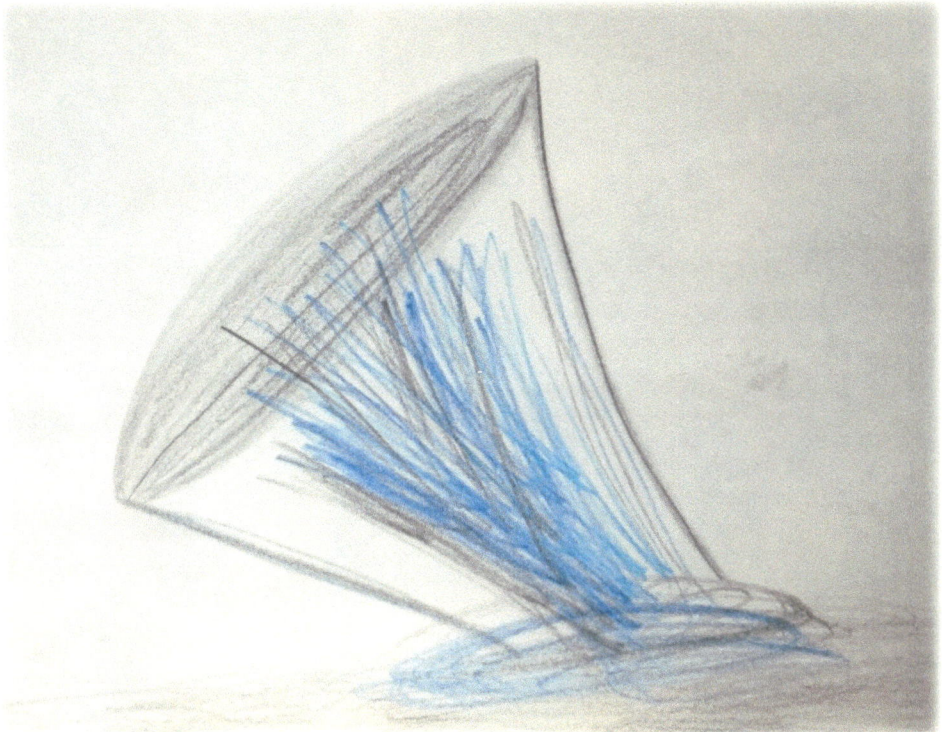

I could see the deep basins. Oh. Little Joey. Were you in a deep basin somewhere in those woods? Had you gotten lost? I hate writing about your death. It is painful to think of a little 9 year old boy alone in those woods…

The anniversary of his death is coming up next month. Oh. It is almost the end of this month. We are getting an extra second so they can reset time. Why do we think we can rest…reset time? We can screw it up and then fix it "next time". Why didn't we do it right the first time? We could have done something different the next time and not had to redo the first time. How many "redos" does the average person have in a lifetime?

The sink. It is about the sink…

He used to stand in front of the sink and watch the water swirling down the drain. Swirling and swirling…

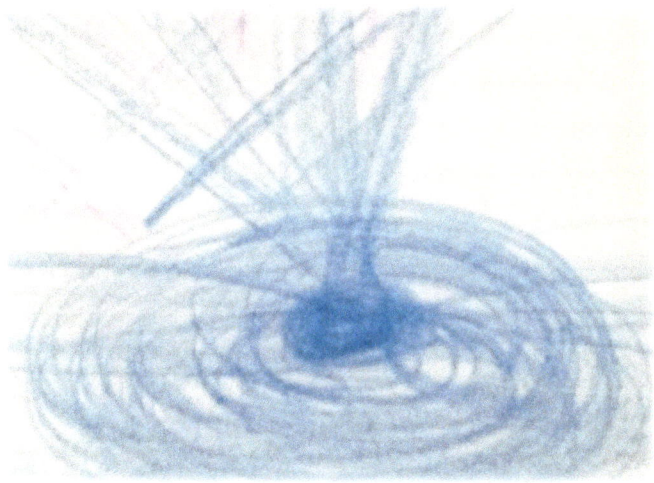

Tony. Make it all go away he used to think. Whatever bad had crossed his day…he would wash it away as the water swirled around…

Clean.

And empty.

The sink would be at the end.

Is that how he felt sometimes? Clean…but empty?

There was a house too. It was a big house. There were paths all around it. They were paved red. This one should have been easy to figure out…

All the different paths to get to the house…

Why red? There is a lot of red. Red flags and red rugs and red paths. Is it just so I will stop and think…

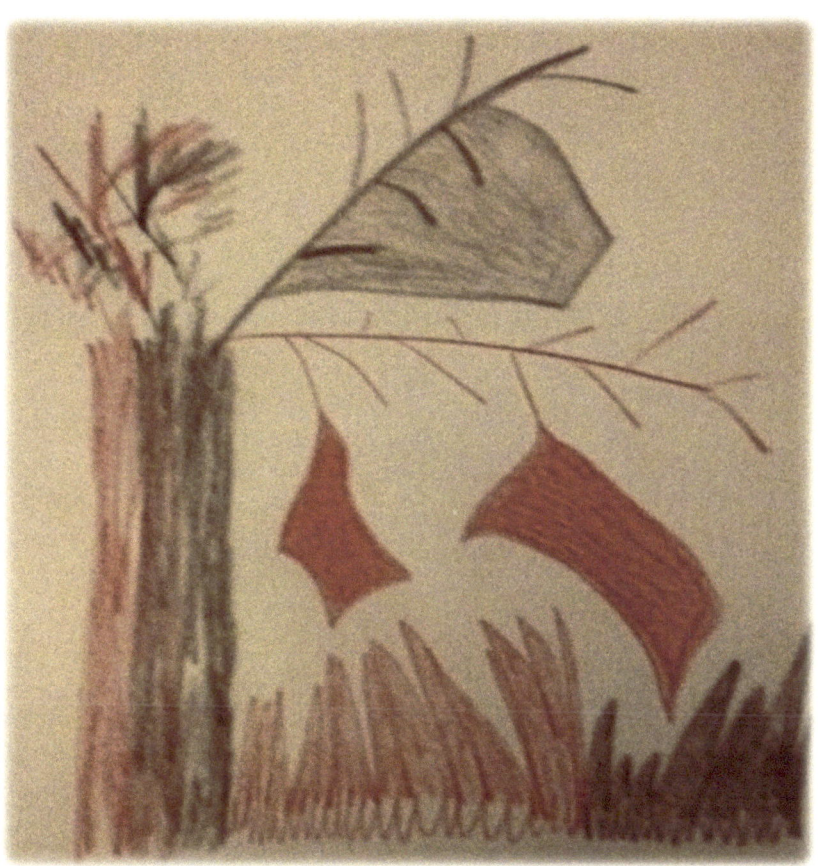

...and think I did. About the things that cannot be explained...

"I love the things that cannot be explained. They challenge us. They strain our minds, bend our hearts, and open our eyes. Even better yet, I love when the unexpected occurs. The unexpected in a mundane life. A life well on its course takes a turn in a direction that a month prior could have never been seen or even dreamed. "Do you believe in spirits?" I asked my friend. "Ghosts, you mean?" he replied. "No…spirits of people who have died." "Well look", he said, "I believe there are things that can't be explained." That was all I needed to hear…and I began to pour out ALL my stories…" Excerpt from "Chapel Street Signs". The beginning.

I will be almost up to 300,000 words by the end of "Hand of Heven".

About the Author and *Illustrator*

RL Lane has published the EcarreT series and a collection of art books featuring the illustrations throughout the books. The series begins with "Chapel Street Signs"…

…unexplained connections that challenge us to beli ve. A woman, a Dad a Doctor, a cat and mouse, a horse and tale tell their stories. "Do you beli ve in spirits?" I asked my friend. "Well look", he said, "I believe there are things that cannot be explained…" Oh. Plus, hear ov a Mom's battle with her struggle to connect to the woman…her little girl.

Welcome to EcarreT…a world
Where everyone cares
Why did I have to create it in…

A fiction fantasy world?

You may already know why, but you will see regardless of what you believe as a girl's journey of love and faith on her "Touring Machine" take her on the best journey of her mundane life. A life well on its way takes a turn in a direction that could've never been seen or even dreamed…

The author can be contacted at:

RosaLeeeLane@gmail.com
www.Amazon.com/author/readrllane

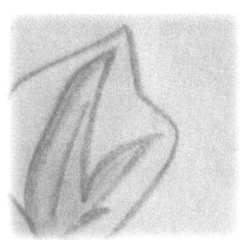